WITH TWELVE ANSWERS TO PROPER MLM SUCCESS

WHAT YOU SHOULD CONSIDER BEFORE INVESTING A LOT OF MONEY AND TIME IN MLM, NETWORK MARKETING OR REFERRAL MARKETING SYSTEMS.

ANNE SCHLOSSER

Contents

Preface   v

  1. Illegal Pyramid Scheme?   1

  2. Twelve Questions That You Should Answer   4
    Before Entering An Mlm System.

  3. Conclusion   16

Disclaimer   17

Preface

Even if I make myself unpopular in the MLM branch with this: 80% of the people that enter an MLM-, network marketing or referral marketing system will never realize just one euro profit and will not even be able to cover their own expenses. Of the remaining 20% approximately one tenth is very successful and is not only able to live from their income, but also to achieve actual prosperity, the remaining nine-tenths earn a more or less big grant that after deduction of their own expenses contributes to their monthly income or they are able to have a modest life with their earnings without the need for another occupation.

I am one of the lucky ones. Admittedly, there is no Ferrari in my garage, but I have become so wealthy with the help of referral marketing that I can live well with just my commission payments; but I am not genuinely rich. Precisely, I can be happy about a monthly income in the lower five-digit region and am very thankful for that. To maintain that, I am publishing this book under a pseudonym because I am aware of the fact that I might get on the wrong side of some people with that.

In my networking career, I have not only learned a lot about the products but also especially about people. In particular, I have found out that with newcomers, that newly enter a network marketing service, I can say with a one hundred percent accuracy whether or not the respective person will be successful with their operation after asking them a few questions.

Since my work time as an executive - but especially also the work time of my partners in my downline is precious - I have decided to write this book. On the basis of twelve questions. With this, I will offer a base to those interested on which they can find out for themselves whether a particular MLM system suits them. I think that this is fair to all concerned. The prospects do not invest unnecessary time and money in a system that will not bring them the desired results and their potential sponsors can concentrate on the promotion and the development of people that will sustainably secure them success and commissions.

If you find out that a certain system does not suit you on the basis of your own answers, it does not mean that there is not the right provider for the development of your income, but only that you possibly might not have found him yet.

I wish you a lot of success with building your passive income

Yours, Anne Schlosser

All of my observations are based on my own experiences. They do not represent advice for your completely specific case and, above all, they do not promise success. The booklet is rather supposed to give you something to think about. As a mature reader, you are responsible for what you make of the described information as well as the gained knowledge.

CHAPTER ONE

ILLEGAL PYRAMID SCHEME?

The question that most people that are active in an MLM have to listen to over and over is the question of whether this is about an illegal pyramid scheme. When I respond to questions like this with what they mean by pyramid scheme, it often turns out that my interlocutor does not really know what that is exactly. Recently, a lady responded: »It is a business that is illegal and dangerous because people lose money with it.«

What is noticeable here is that the issue »pyramid scheme« is not really addressed regarding its »definition«, but rather that the issue is addressed with the topic of its alleged »illegality«. For this reason, let me go back a little further.

Are MLM systems, network marketing or referral marketing illegal?

Basically, one can answer that with a clear »no«. Nevertheless, it is imaginable that an organization that operates an illegal business can also do this with the help

1

of an MLM system. Respective examples have been there in the past. To project that onto a whole branch is just as precipitately as if you deemed pizza parlors, car dealers, nurseries, doctors or taxi companies criminal just because there do exist black sheep in these industries and sectors as well.

When is an MLM system illegal?

Basically, the business of every company is illegal if it violates the law with its operations. If a company, regardless of MLM or not, for example, sells not permitted, banned fireworks, they are illegal - regardless, of whether the law is based on MLM or not. In the field of network marketing, there is an additional rule that stated that an MLM system is against the law when the central source of income of the members does not come from selling products or services, but for the most part from recruiting new »players«. This is not the case with legitimate MLM systems. Usually, with reputable sellers, it is rather the case that there is a producer of one or more products whose focus is on putting the products on the market with the help of an alternative chain of distribution. With this, the usual included wholesale and retail markup is paid instead of the trade with the people in the MLM structure.

Can I lose money with MLM Geld?

The answer is very clear: »Yes, you can«. As in every business you, also with MLM, invest money in the purchase of products, possibly also in the participation in further education or similar services and you can lose this money when your business is not successful. It is about business and that always includes a certain risk.

However, with most MLM systems this is very manageable. Many systems do not even know an entry fee or only a minimal entry fee and they only know the obligation to purchase the necessary products that they need for themselves for little money in order to be fully commissionable. If one compares that to some franchise systems where the right to establish a subsidiary of the respective franchiser has to be bought with ten thousand or even hundred thousands of euro, then the risk with most of the MLM systems is quite calculable and affordable for most of the people in our region.

To reduce your risk, I have written this booklet. With answering the following twelve questions you can find a good basis of decision-making for yourself to determine whether or not a particular system is promising for your success. If you do not know an answer to some of the questions, ask your sponsor. A good, experienced sponsor should be able to answer all of the answers without a problem.

CHAPTER TWO

TWELVE QUESTIONS THAT YOU SHOULD ANSWER BEFORE ENTERING AN MLM SYSTEM.

Divestment or recommendation?

Every MLM operation has something to do with selling. Only if there is a person that is willing to pay for a product, sales are pulled in with which commissions can be paid. Much more accurate it would be to say that, on the one side, there are MLM systems where reduced products are purchased and then sold to customers. On the other side, there are those where you recommend or sell products to a prospect without having the product on hand yourself because they are send to the customer directly by the producer and you just get a fee in the end or a success commission.

Also important with systems in which you sell on your own, is the question: Are there any sales restrictions or conditions in your country that you have to fulfill in order to sell certain products yourself? As far as products in the medical or medical-related field are concerned: Are these approved in your country at all?

Questions that you should ask yourself:

I often get to know people that enter the MLM business but do not have sales success because they are not good at approaching people. Usually, this is not about persuading people, but to do them something good. Honestly, ask yourself the following questions:

- Am I confident and excited enough of the products of the provider that I would also recommend it to my friends out of conviction?
- Do I like to approach others and talk to them?
- Can I sell or am ready to learn it?
- Are the offered products expellable within the law in my country? What requirements must I literally meet and which liability risks do I possibly have to take?

It may well be that, based on your current state of information, you are not able to answer some of the questions by yourself. In this case, it is advisable to talk them through with your potential sponsor. He should also have an interest in you making conscious decisions because only then you will continue with your plan in the long term and bring him revenue in the long run.

Buying into the system?

Almost every provider has put up an entry barrier for new sales partners. This barrier can be varyingly difficult to overcome depending on the strategy of the company. There are providers where the price for entering is that you actually consume the products yourself. This seems to make sense to me because if you actually use the products, you can best provide information about them. But some systems require a minimum initial order amount or the purchase of a franchise bunch or something similar.

Questions that you should ask yourself:

- What sales do you have to realize in order to compensate the investment in buying into the system? How long do you need for that? (For comparison, ask your sponsor how long he needed for that.)
- Which services do you purchase when buying into the system and what would you have to pay for similar services »on the free market«?
- What is the proportion of your price you have to pay to enter the system regarding the prices and winning possibilities through selling the products. If the price you need to pay is inadequate to the mentioned willing possibilities, this could be a sign for the presence of an illegal pyramid scheme.
- What will happen after you bought yourself into the system? How does your system support you (and your sponsor) with accomplishing your own successes?

Selling products or building system?

Most of the MLM or network marketing programs know two levels on which their partners can generate revenues. Firstly, revenues that are based on own sales own recommendations or placement of the products or services. Secondly, revenues that are achieved by attracting further partners that in turn generate with the respective products and services on their own. If you enter MLM, you are taking an important step towards becoming an entrepreneur (for now probably part-time or side-line entrepreneur). Take the first step in this direction by asking yourself the following questions:

Questions that you should ask yourself:

- Should I rather focus on selling the products or on attracting new partners or on a combination of both? What are the advantages/ disadvantages for me?
- Did I understand the compensation plan? What compensation do I get for my own sales, what compensation for the sales from partners on different levels, what commission do I get for attracting new partners, etc.?

Minimum purchase / minimum sales?

Some systems know certain minimum purchases or minimum sales in order to get commission, to keep their self-built structure, etc. In other words, there are MLM systems where you are overtaken by partners that you initially attracted if you do not generate more sales than they do. That means, you suddenly do not get commissions from your »pick of the bunch« and its downline anymore. We all like to imagine the situation where everything works out and where we walk through the streets of Hollywood as »future millionaires«. Nevertheless, it is important, especially with a decision, to think about what will happen when something does not work out and one, for example, cannot be as active anymore because of health-related reasons.

Questions that you should ask yourself:

- Does a minimum sales clause exist?
- Which one and how high is it? Am I sure that I can fulfill it in any case?
- What happens if I do not achieve minimum sales (once, repeatedly, for a lengthy period of time)?

Consequences of vacation, absence, illness?

In the same context is the question of what happens with your revenue and your downline, hence, to the sales partners and customers that you attracted, when you go on vacation or if you because of other reasons cannot be active for a limited period of time or even for a longer period of time. Different from when you are employed, as someone with an own business you are responsible for ensuring your revenues. As long as you only do network marketing as a »hobby« this might not be too important. But if you plan on paying a partial amount of or your whole subsistence with the respective revenues, then it is essential that you think about this early enough.

Question that you should ask yourself:

- What will happen with my revenues and my position in the system if I do not achieve sales or significantly fewer sales for a longer time?

- Are there any time limits that I have to consider and be aware of?
- Can I pass on or sell my position as the circumstances require (as in a company)?
- Are there rules after which period of time of inactivity or not achieving certain goals I »get kicked out of the system«?

Authenticity?

Imagine Mr. X. He smokes like a chimney and knows exercise only from the dictionary. Mr. X. offers you health products or vital substances. What would you think of that? Is there any chance you would ask yourself why Mr. X. apparently does not consume his own products or if he does consume them, what is wrong with them? Just as reluctantly you would order a face cream from a lady that has a bad skin. It may well be that the blemished skin has very different reasons and that Mr. X has only survived smoking that much because of consuming the vital substances. But the potential customer will probably look at that differently.

Questions that you should ask yourself:

- Can I offer the products reliably without telling any potential customer half of my life story?
- Would I buy the offered products from myself if I were stranger or an acquaintance? It can be quite useful to ask this question to an acquaintance. But he should be someone that tells you the truth even if it might be unpleasant.

- How do the products suit me and my image? Of course, you can also sell products that do not suit your image. But it is much easier if you are already perceived as an expert or as someone that already knows something about the respective field by your environment before you start selling the products.

Redemption of the goods?

When you purchase the products from the producer or its sales company for reselling purposes or for your own requirements, it may happen that you have overestimated yourself. Or, you realize that a bought product does not meet your expectations. But in most cases you have already paid at this time.

Questions that you should ask yourself:

- Can these products be returned?
- Can already open packages be returned if you or the customer should not be satisfied?
- Which time limits or other provisions should be considered?
- How are returned goods compensated? (money back, credit advice, replacement, only a part of the money is given back ...)

Product quality / liability?

The mere fact that a product can be legally purchased somewhere in this world does not mean that this also has to apply to your country. There are certainly countries where cannabis products can be sold legally. But that does not mean that you would not be guilty of an offense if you built your own little hemp plantation if you owned respective products for purchase or even offered them for sale. In addition, there is always the question of liability, especially then when you sell the products. Are you able to determine whether your product really helps your potential customer or if it might even harm him? As long as you tell someone your experiences with the product, that should not present a problem. But what happens if you sell a product to someone who does not tolerate it for some reason? Especially in the context of health products the path is quite narrow, especially, if it is not only about nutritional supplements, but products that are classified as remedies by the local legislative power.

Questions that you should ask yourself:

- Is it legal in your country to sell the products you want to sell?
- Which evidence do you have for the quality of the offered product?
- Do you have liability and legal costs insurance or does it include issues like this? Attention: usually private insurances do not or hardly cover business-related activities.
- If the offered products should not be approved in your country: why not? Because they are not approvable or because they are not approved because of any other convictions?

What does »the State« demand from me?

What many MLM entrepreneurs do not take into account is the question of social coverage. On the one side, in most countries it is the case that revenues from own businesses have to be tax paid, but in many cases are subjected to further fees, such as social insurance, occupational pension, etc. If the income has reached a certain amount of money. Especially MLM entrepreneurs do often not think of the fact that they have to meet certain governmental obligations even with relatively low sales. The ancient wisdom »ignorance is no excuse in law« does also apply here. In any case, it is advisable to inform oneself in advance about which legal requirements exist in your field and in your case.

Questions that you should ask yourself:

- At what revenue do I have to register my occupation as a business or the like?
- What provisions exist regarding accounting?
- How are further fees regulated in my case: social insurance, insurances, taxes?
- What support does my MLM organization offer with that or which requirements does it perhaps have itself?

Willingness to improve one's knowledge?

A very central feature does distinguish successful network marketers from unsuccessful ones. Who wants to be successful in this branch, has to continuously better oneself. Many providers organize such further training, often with top orators for very little money, some do even stipulate a certain minimum of training before they allowed you to become active for your own company.

Further, training usually takes place in the field of professional development (product knowledge, knowledge in the subject area) that is supposed to help you to communicate about the product in a skilled way and to make you seem competent in front of a potential customer.

Besides that, many network marketing companies increasingly focus on the training of the participants in the area of personality development. Common topics are self-confidence, sales training, communication, etc. Of course, these further trainings do not only offer a big potential for sales success, but also the personality development.

Questions that you should ask yourself:

- Am I willing to study further in both events as well as with reading and in contact with my sponsor or with the trainer of the organization?
- What temporal effort am I willing to schedule?

Cooperation with your sponsor?

A successful MLM carrier is in the most cases based on a positive cooperation with your sponsor. Only if you have good contact and if your sponsor is active himself and works on himself and his downline, he will be able to support you with reaching your goals. This will bring him an invaluable financial advantage, he, therefore, does not only help you out of the goodness of his heart. Unfortunately, I have seen how network marketing beginners failed because their sponsor was a »lazy dog« who left them alone once he had the »signed contract« in his pocket.

Questions that you should ask yourself:

- Can I/ Do I want to intensively work together with my sponsor for a longer time?
- Which support does my sponsor offer?
- Ask your sponsor if he can name you some customers that he has attracted and absolutely ask them back about your sponsor.
- How successful is your sponsor? If he promises you prosperity within a short time, but obviously does not have enough money for a cup of coffee, you should consider whether his statements are credible.

Time budget and willingness to go the extra mile?

Especially at the beginning of your MLM carrier, you will have to spend a lot of time. You can handle it this way only for a short time, but also over a longer period of time. In most cases it will take quite some time until notable successes are achieved and only very few people accomplish it to become wealthy within months (certainly, such cases exist.) But also, these mostly work very hard for it. If one could earn money in the MLM sector in one's sleep, most people in referral marketing would be successful.

Questions that you should ask yourself:

- How much time am I willing and able to invest into building my MLM carrier (further education, making contacts, having sales and sponsoring talks)?
- How much effort does my sponsor make and how long did it take him to, for example, get a monthly commission of 1000 euro (if he already makes that

much)?

- Also, actively ask your sponsor what he would want as a time investment and agree upon your possibilities. In most organizations it is no problem if you have only very little time, especially in MLM one can organize everything. You have to be aware of the fact that »hard times« can be longer, depending on how much time and effort you are able to put into your business. With this, it is important to honestly discuss this point with your sponsor in order to prevent possible disapproval and misunderstandings because both assume different ideas.

CHAPTER THREE

CONCLUSION

Although it is often spoken about a passive income in network marketing, not all providers keep this promise. What all systems have in common is that only those are successful who are also willing to show the appropriate commitment. I myself am the best proof that you can achieve a certain wealth with network marketing and believe me, I know people that have become really rich with it. But what they all have in common is that the success did not just drop into their laps. They have rather worked hard for it for a long time, albeit self-determined, as their »own boss«.

I think it is very important in the MLM branch that people decide for or against it consciously. People that are lured with false promises are dissatisfied and harm the entire industry. Besides that, such people - and this is not meant as a judgment - are useless for the sponsor as well.

Especially in this branch, it is of crucial importance to invest one's power in the partners that are skilled, willing and ready to show the respective commitment and effort. Everything else will just hold the sponsor back.

Disclaimer

Introduction

By using this book, you accept this disclaimer in full.

No advice

The book contains information. The information is not advice, and should not be treated as such.

If you think you may be suffering from any medical condition you should seek immediate medical attention. You should never delay seeking medical advice, disregard medical advice, or discontinue medical treatment because of information in the book.

No representations or warranties

To the maximum extent permitted by applicable law and subject to section below, we exclude all representations, warranties, undertakings and guarantees relating to the book.

Without prejudice to the generality of the foregoing paragraph, we do not represent, warrant, undertake or guarantee:

- that the information in the book is correct, accurate, complete or non-misleading;

- that the use of the guidance in the book will lead to any particular outcome or result.

Limitations and exclusions of liability

The limitations and exclusions of liability set out in this section and elsewhere in this disclaimer: are subject to section 6 below; and govern all liabilities arising under the disclaimer or in relation to the book, including liabilities arising in contract, in tort (including negligence) and for breach of statutory duty.

We will not be liable to you in respect of any losses arising out of any event or events beyond our reasonable control.

We will not be liable to you in respect of any business losses, including without limitation loss of or damage to profits, income, revenue, use, production, anticipated savings, business, contracts, commercial opportunities or goodwill.

We will not be liable to you in respect of any loss or corruption of any data, database or software.

We will not be liable to you in respect of any special, indirect or consequential loss or damage.

Exceptions

Nothing in this disclaimer shall: limit or exclude our liability for death or personal injury resulting from negligence; limit or exclude our liability for fraud or fraudulent misrepresentation; limit any of our liabilities in any way that is not permitted under applicable law; or exclude any of our liabilities that may not be excluded under applicable law.

Severability

If a section of this disclaimer is determined by any court or other competent authority to be unlawful and/or unenforceable, the other sections of this disclaimer continue in effect.

If any unlawful and/or unenforceable section would be lawful or enforceable if part of it were deleted, that part will be deemed to be deleted, and the rest of the section will continue in effect.

Law and jurisdiction

DISCLAIMER

This disclaimer will be governed by and construed in accordance with Swiss law, and any disputes relating to this disclaimer will be subject to the exclusive jurisdiction of the courts of Switzerland.